Spiralizer Cookbook

Top 50 Healthy and Delicious Recipes for You and Your Family

Table of Contents

Introduction

Did you just find out about the spiralizer and are wondering what you can do with it, and *why* you would even want to use one? Well, this book is going to teach you how to use a spiralizer and why you want to use one.

Spiralizers are handheld devices used to transform vegetables and fruits into spaghetti, rice, or just sliced for convenience. Instead of using pasta in your next spaghetti and meatball dinner, why not use spiralized zucchini or sweet potato?

Take a look at the following benefits of using a spiralizer.

Assists Weight Loss

Spiralizing is an amazing way to introduce more vegetables and fruits into your diet. Spiralized veggies are naturally low calorie, low carb, low sugar, high fibre and unprocessed. These are some of the most critical elements of weight loss. The high fibre and water content of veggies also promotes that feeling of fullness that is so important in not starving yourself!

Gluten-Free

If you are on a Paleo diet, or you would like to stay gluten-free for medical reasons, then eating wheat-free products is already a way to support your dietary needs. But if you are tired of trying to consume gluten-free substitutes like gluten-free flour, then why not try spiralizing? You can make vegetable noodles and rice in no time!

Eat More to Get Enough Calories

That is right, you did not read that wrong. You have probably never had someone tell you to eat more, but with spiralized vegetables, you should eat more to get the amount of calories you need. Just think about it, instead of eating only two hardboiled eggs in the morning to get the calories you need for the rest of the day, why not eat a hardboiled egg *and* a bowl of zucchini noodles? The noodles are a lot more filling than the eggs because of the amount of fiber they have, and this helps you stay feeling fuller for longer than just two eggs.

Food Goes Further

We eat with our eyes. Not really, we actually begin eating our food before it even touches our mouths. And when you have a tiny bowl of chopped zucchini or sweet potato in front of you, it is disappointing. But if you spiralize your zucchini or potato, you get a lot more 'volume' in your bowl or on your plate, and that will make you feel satisfied before you even begin chowing down!

Convenient

Not only is spiralizing a time-saver when it comes to making pasta with vegetables, but it will also make it a lot easier to feed your kids vegetables! And all this is thanks to lovely, bright, long or short, multi-colored and highly luscious spirals on your table...

In addition to that, spiralizing does not require electricity. You can get a manual spiralizer for when the power goes out and you will not have to worry about not being able to use it. It also stores nicely with your other appliances.

Variety

Spiralizing is an ideal way of making various healthy and unique dishes. Instead of just creating a pasta dish, you can create over twenty different types of vegetable noodles! So instead of having to eat just one type of pasta, you could combine spiralized vegetables to make a beautiful, colorful pasta dish.

There are so many benefits to using a spiralizer to make your meals. Not only is it nutritious, but also it saves you time and money.

So start spiralizing today with the recipes in this cookbook and keep in mind that one of the main priorities of spiralizing is opting for healthy food!

Roasted Vegetable Noodles

Prep time: 15 minutes | Cook time: 20 minutes | Serves 6

Ingredients:
- 1 medium zucchini
- 1 medium summer squash
- 1 large carrot
- 1 small sweet potato
- 4 oz. red onion
- 6 oz. mixed bell peppers (red, yellow, and green)
- 3 large cloves garlic
- 3 tbsp. bacon fat or butter
- Salt and pepper, to taste

Directions:
1. Preheat oven to 400° F.
2. Grease a baking sheet with the bacon fat or butter.
3. Using a vegetable spiralizer, slice the squash, zucchini, sweet potato, and carrot into ribbons.
4. Run the bell peppers, red onion, and garlic through a mandolin.
5. Add to the spiraled vegetables, season with salt and pepper and toss to combine.
6. Place the vegetable noodles on the prepared baking sheet, spread with hands and cook in the oven for 15-20 minutes, tossing with a fork 2-3 times.

Indian Carrot Noodle Salad with Spiced Lamb

Prep time: 20 minutes | *Cook time: 15 minutes* | *Serves 2*

Ingredients:
- 1 lb. (450 g) lamb, ground lean
- 2 tsp. garam masala
- Salt, to taste
- 3 large carrots, peeled and spiralized
- ¼ cup fresh cilantro
- ¼ cup fresh mint

For the dressing:
- ½ tsp. dried cumin
- 1 small red onion, peeled and sliced thinly
- Zest and juice of 1 lemon
- 1 tsp. freshly grated ginger
- 4 tbsp. extra virgin olive oil

Directions:

1. Place a large frying pan on the stove and let it heat over medium heat.
2. Once very hot, add the ground lamb to the pan and crumble with a wooden spoon.
3. Next, stir in the garam masala and season with salt and pepper to taste.
4. Once the lamb becomes golden brown and crispy, remove the pan from the heat.
5. To make carrot noodles, run the peeled carrots through a vegetable spiralizer and place in a large bowl. Add the chopped mint and cilantro.
6. In a small bowl, mix together the onion, cumin, lemon juice and zest, olive oil, and ginger.
7. Pour the dressing over the carrots and toss well to coat.
8. Place the cooked lamb on serving plates, top with carrot salad, and enjoy.

Raw Beetroot Salad with Walnut Dressing

Prep time: 30 minutes | Total time: 15 minutes | Serves 1-2

Ingredients:
- 2 medium raw beets
- 1 medium carrot
- 4-5 slices of goat cheese, crumbled

For the dressing:
- ¼ cup walnuts
- ¼ cup extra virgin olive oil
- 2 tbsp. lemon juice
- 1 small garlic clove, finely diced
- ½ tsp. maple syrup or honey
- ¼ tsp. sea salt
- Pinch of pepper

Directions:
1. Peel beetroots and carrots and run through a vegetable spiralizer. Place the vegetable noodles in a bowl.
2. Combine the walnuts, lemon juice, olive oil, garlic, maple syrup or honey, salt, and pepper in a blender and pulse until walnuts are finely chopped.
3. Pour about 3 tablespoons of dressing over the noodles and toss to coat.
4. Sprinkle with goat cheese and enjoy.

Cashew Pesto Pasta with Spring Vegetables

Prep time: 40 minutes | Cook time: 20 minutes | Serves 4

Ingredients:

- 1 cup asparagus pieces
- 4 medium zucchini, peeled and spiralized
- 2 oz. prosciutto
- 2 tbsp. virgin olive oil
- 8 oz. cremini mushrooms, roughly chopped
- ½ cup cherry tomatoes, cut in half
- 1 cup raw cashews
- 2 tbsp. basil, chopped
- 4 cups boiling water
- 1 tbsp. lemon juice
- Dash of white pepper
- Dash of nutmeg
- 1 garlic clove
- ¼ tsp. salt
- Garnish with toasted pine nuts and fresh basil

Directions:

1. Place the cashews in a pot of 4 cups boiling water and let stand for 30 minutes.
2. Meanwhile, place the zucchini noodles in a large saucepan of boiling of water and let blanch for 1-2 minutes.
3. Then quickly transfer to a colander and rinse under cold running water.

4. Place the zucchini noodles on a platter lined with kitchen towel to drain and set aside.
5. Then, in the same saucepan, cook the asparagus until crisp-tender.
6. Drain in the colander and set aside.
7. Add the olive oil to a medium skillet and set over medium heat.
8. Add the mushrooms and prosciutto and fry for 4-5 minutes. Then turn the heat to low and start making the sauce.
9. Reserving the soaking water, drain the cashews in the colander and place in a blender. Add 1 cup of the soaking water, basil, lemon juice, garlic, nutmeg, salt, and pepper, and pulse until smooth.
10. Add the asparagus and sauce to the skillet with prosciutto and mushrooms and cook for 10 minutes.
11. Add the tomatoes and remove the skillet from heat.
12. Place the zucchini in a serving plate, top with the sauce, sprinkle with toasted pine nuts and fresh basil, and enjoy.

Healthy Vegetable Pasta with Carrot, Zucchini, and Squash

Prep time: 10 minutes | Cook time: 5 minutes | Serves 4

Ingredients:
- 1 medium carrot, spiraled
- 2 medium yellow squash, spiraled
- 2 medium zucchini, spiraled
- 1 tbsp. extra virgin olive oil
- ¼ cup red onion, diced
- 3 garlic cloves, minced
- Salt and fresh cracked pepper, to taste

Directions:
1. Run your carrots, zucchini, and squash through a vegetable spiralizer and set aside.
2. Add the oil to a frying pan and set over medium heat.
3. Add the onions and garlic and sauté for about 1 to 2 minutes, until aromatic.
4. Add the spiraled zucchini, squash, and carrots to the pan and cook for 3-4 minutes over medium-high heat.
5. Sprinkle with salt and pepper and give a stir to combine flavors. Adjust seasonings to taste.
6. Remove from the heat and serve immediately.

Chicken and Chickpea Broccoli Noodle Pasta

Prep time: 15 minutes | Cook time: 20 minutes | Serves 3

Ingredients:
- 5 tbsp. extra virgin olive oil
- 1 boneless chicken breast
- Salt and pepper, to taste
- ¼ tsp. dried oregano flakes
- 2 broccoli stems, spiralized
- ½ cup canned chickpeas, drained and rinsed
- ½ cup green peas, cooked
- ½ cup leeks, thinly sliced

For the dressing:
- 2 tbsp. basil, chopped
- 1/3 cup feta
- ½ shallot, chopped
- 1 tbsp. lemon juice
- Salt and pepper, to taste
- 1 tbsp. olive oil
- 1 tbsp. red wine vinegar
- 1 small garlic clove, minced

Directions:

1. Season the chicken with salt and pepper, and sprinkle with oregano flakes.
2. Add the olive oil to a large frying pan and set over medium heat.
3. Once the oil begins to sizzle, add the chicken and let cook for about 7-8 minutes. Remove from the pan and set aside.
4. Add the peas and broccoli noodles to a saucepan of boiling water and let cook for 3 minutes until the peas become bright green and broccoli is crisp tender. Drain in a colander and let cool for 2-3 minutes.
5. Meanwhile, combine the basil, feta, shallot, lemon juice, olive oil, vinegar, garlic, salt, and pepper in a blender and pulse until smooth and creamy.
6. Place the canned chickpeas, cooked peas, broccoli noodles, and leeks in a large bowl. Cut the chicken and add to the bowl. Spoon the dressing over and mix well to combine. Enjoy.

Zucchini Noodles with Chicken, Feta, and Spinach

Prep time: 5 minutes | Cook time: 10 minutes | Serves 1

Ingredients:
- 1 large zucchini, spiralized
- Juice of half a lemon
- 1 packed cup of spinach
- Pinch of red pepper flakes
- ½ tsp. garlic powder
- 2-3 chicken breast tenderloins (strips), cut into chunks
- 5 small cubes of feta cheese (less than ¼ cup)
- Salt and pepper, to taste

Directions:
1. Place a large skillet over medium heat and add chicken.
2. Season with salt and pepper and let cook for about 3 minutes and then flip over, cooking another 3-5 minutes, until the chicken is cooked through.
3. Add in the lemon juice, spinach, zucchini, and garlic powder. Let cook about 3 minutes.
4. Use pasta tongs to transfer to a bowl.
5. Season with pepper, top with feta, and enjoy.

Zucchini Noodles with Shrimp

Prep time: 10 minutes | *Cook time: 15 minutes* | *Serves 4*

Ingredients:
- 2 large zucchini, spiralized
- 1 tbsp. olive oil
- 1 small onion, chopped
- 4 garlic cloves, minced
- 1 tsp. hot sauce of your choice
- 1 cup cherry tomatoes, cut in half
- 1 cup chicken broth
- Juice from half a lemon
- ½ cup parmesan cheese
- 1 lb. cooked shrimp

Directions:
1. Heat the olive oil in a large skillet and cook the onion and garlic until soft.
2. Add hot sauce, chicken broth, and juice from half a lemon.
3. Stir then throw in the shrimp and cherry tomatoes.
4. Cook for a couple minutes, but not too long because shrimp is already cooked.
5. Season with salt and pepper.
6. Remove from heat and add zucchini noodles. Mix to combine.
7. Sprinkle with green onions and Parmesan cheese. Serve while warm. Enjoy.

Mediterranean Pasta

Prep time: 5 minutes │ Cook time: 5 minutes │ Serves 4

Ingredients:

- 2 tbsp. olive oil
- 2 tbsp. butter
- 2 large zucchinis, spiralized
- 1 cup spinach, packed
- 5 garlic cloves, minced
- ¼ cup sun-dried tomatoes
- 2 tbsp. capers
- 2 tbsp. parsley, chopped
- 10 Kalamata olives, halved
- ¼ cup feta cheese, crumbled
- ¼ cup parmesan cheese, shredded
- Salt and pepper, to taste

Directions:

1. Add the butter and olive oil to a large skillet over medium heat. Add the garlic and sauté for 30 seconds, until fragrant.
2. Add the zucchini noodles and spinach, season with salt and pepper, and cook until the zucchini becomes soft and spinach is wilts.
3. Add the capers, sun-dried tomatoes, Kalamata olives, parsley, and cook for another 3 minutes, stirring frequently.
4. Sprinkle the dish with feta and Parmesan cheeses and serve.

Spiralized Cabbage with Tuna and Almonds

Prep time: 5 minutes | Cook time: 5 minutes | Serves 3

Ingredients:
- 1 head of cabbage, spiralized
- 1 tbsp. olive oil
- 2 garlic cloves, minced
- 1 pinch red pepper flakes
- ½ cup diced red onion
- 1/3 cup low-sodium chicken broth
- 2 cans chunky light tuna (in water)
- 2 tbsp. slivered or sliced almonds
- Salt and pepper, to taste

Directions:
1. Place a large skillet over medium heat and add in the olive oil.
2. Add in the garlic and red pepper flakes. Let cook for 30 seconds.
3. Add in the onion. Cook for 2 minutes.
4. Add in the cabbage and season with salt and pepper.
5. Cook the cabbage, tossing frequently, for about 2 minutes and then add in the chicken broth. Let reduce fully.
6. Add in the tuna and toss to combine, letting cook for about 1 minute to heat up.
7. Divide cabbage and tuna mixture into bowls and top with almonds. Enjoy!

Carrot Risotto with Bacon

Prep time: 10 minutes | *Cook time: 20 minutes* | *Serves 1*

Ingredients:
- 2 slices of bacon
- 2 medium carrots, peeled and spiralized
- 1 tsp. garlic, minced
- ½ cup of sliced leeks
- ½ cup plus 1 tbsp. low-sodium vegetable broth
- 1 tbsp. fresh lemon juice
- Pepper, to taste
- Cooking spray
- 1 tsp. freshly chopped parsley, to garnish

Directions:
1. Coat a frying pan with cooking spray and set over medium heat.
2. Place the bacon slices in the pan and roast until crispy and lightly brown on all sides.
3. Remove from the pan and place on a plate lined with paper towel.
4. Spiralize the carrots and then throw into a food processor. Process for about 10 seconds until the carrots are finely chopped into rice-size pieces. Set aside.
5. Add the garlic and leeks to the same pan where the bacon has been cooked and which is still coated with bacon fat. Stir-fry for about a minute, then add 1 tablespoon of vegetable

broth.

6. Cook for a few seconds, stirring, and then add the carrot "rice" and lemon juice.
7. Sprinkle with pepper and stir to combine. After a minute, add the remaining vegetable broth.
8. Let cook until all liquid is absorbed and the carrots become tender, about 8-10 minutes.
9. Let cook for 1 minute and then add in the rest of the vegetable broth. Let cook until the liquid is fully absorbed.
10. Cut the fried bacon into thin slices and add to the carrot "rice". Mix to combine.
11. Place the dish in a serving bowl, sprinkle with chopped parsley, and serve.

Carrot Fettuccine with Mushrooms and Red Pepper

Prep time: 10 minutes │ *Cook time: 15 minutes* │ *Serves 1*

Ingredients:

- 1 ½ tbsp. olive oil
- 3 large carrots, peeled
- ½ cup diced red bell pepper
- 2 tbsp. fresh basil, chopped
- ½ cup baby bella mushrooms, sliced
- ½ cup cherry tomatoes, quartered
- ¾ cup marinara sauce
- 1 garlic clove, minced
- ½ tbsp. fresh basil, chopped, for garnish
- Salt and pepper, to taste
- Parmesan cheese, to garnish (optional)

Directions:

1. Add the olive oil to a large skillet and place over low heat.
2. Add the red pepper, mushrooms, garlic, and 2 tablespoons of the fresh basil and cook for 3-4 minutes.
3. Stir in the tomatoes, and cook for another 6 minutes, covered.
4. Meanwhile, slice the carrots into ribbons with a vegetable spiral slicer and add to the skillet.
5. Stir in the marinara sauce and cook until the carrots are to your desired doneness.
6. Place the carrot "pasta" into a bowl, garnish with ½ tablespoon of chopped fresh basil, sprinkle with Parmesan cheese, and enjoy.

Zucchini Pasta with Bacon and Shrimps

Prep time: 10 minutes │ Cook time: 15 minutes │ Serves 2

Ingredients:
- 2-3 medium zucchinis, peeled and spiraled
- 1 garlic clove, minced
- 2 pieces of bacon
- 1 pinch red pepper flakes
- ¼ cup minced shallots
- 12 shrimps, defrosted, deveined, and shells removed
- 2 tbsp. freshly chopped parsley
- 4 tbsp. freshly squeezed lemon juice
- 2 tsp. lemon zest
- Salt and pepper, to taste

Directions:
1. Place the bacon in a large frying pan and cook over medium heat, 3 minutes per side, until coated with golden crust.
2. Line a plate with a paper towel and place the roasted bacon onto it.
3. Remove the bacon fat from the pan, reserving about 1 tablespoon of it.
4. Heat the pan over medium heat and cook the garlic for a few seconds.
5. Then add the shallots, shrimp, and red pepper flakes. Flavor with salt and pepper and cook for about 3 minutes, then flip over to cook the other

side as well.

6. Add the lemon zest and juice and cook for another 2 minutes.
7. Remove from the pan, using a slotted spoon.
8. Place the zucchini noodles in the same pan and sauté for 1-2 minutes.
9. Break up the bacon with a fork and add to the noodles. Add the shrimp and mix to combine.
10. Place the dish in 2 serving plates, sprinkle with chopped parsley, and enjoy.

Cucumber Noodles with Asparagus

Prep time: 20 minutes │ Cook time: 2 minutes │ Serves 2-4

Ingredients:

- 2-3 small scallions, thinly sliced
- 2 English cucumbers, peeled
- 1 tsp. toasted sesame oil
- One 2-3 inch piece of fresh ginger, peeled and grated
- 2 tbsp. olive oil
- 1 ½ tbsp. gluten-free tamari or coconut aminos
- 1/8 tsp. red pepper flakes
- Pinch of sea salt, to taste
- 1 bunch asparagus, thinly sliced on the diagonal
- 2 tbsp. toasted sesame seeds, to garnish

Directions:

1. Place the ginger, toasted sesame seeds, scallions, coconut aminos, olive oil, and red pepper flakes in a small bowl. Season with a pinch of salt. Set aside.
2. Place the asparagus in a pot of salted boiling water and let cook for 2 minutes until soft, but still al dente.
3. Pour off the boiling water and add ice water. Let stand for a few minutes.
4. Run the peeled cucumbers through a vegetable spiralizer to create long spiral noodles.

5. Place the cucumbers in a large bowl, and add the blanched and drained asparagus.
6. Pour the ginger sauce over the vegetables and toss to combine.
7. Garnish the dish with sesame seeds and serve.

Chicken Meatballs and Zucchini Pasta

Prep time: 10 minutes | Cook time: 30 minutes | Serves 4

Ingredients:

- ½ cup parmesan cheese, grated
- 1 ½ lbs. (750 g) chicken, ground
- ½ cup fresh basil leaves, finely sliced
- 4 green onions, finely sliced
- Juice and zest of 1 lemon
- 2 tbsp. olive oil
- 1 brown onion, diced
- 2 garlic cloves, thinly sliced
- 2 x 14 oz. (400 g) cans of tomatoes, chopped
- 1 ½ cups chicken broth/water
- 4 zucchini, spiraled
- Parmesan, finely grated
- Handful of basil leaves, to serve

Directions:

8. In a large bowl, add the ground chicken, green onions, parmesan cheese, lemon zest, lemon juice, and chopped basil. Season with salt and pepper and mix well to combine.
9. Shape the mixture into small meatballs and arrange onto a platter.
10. Transfer to the refrigerator and let stand for at least 15 minutes.
11. Add the olive oil to a griddle and set over medium heat. Add the garlic, and onion, and

sauté until tender and golden brown, about 3-4 minutes.

12. Add the canned tomatoes and chicken broth, season with a pinch of black pepper and bring the mixture to a boil.

13. Add the chilled meatballs to the sauce, reduce the heat, and let simmer for about 30 minutes, until the meatballs are cooked well and the tomato sauce has thickened.

14. In the meantime, using a vegetable spiralizer, slice the zucchini into noodles.

15. Place the zucchini pasta into a serving plate, and top with chicken meatballs. Serve sprinkled with grated parmesan and basil leaves.

Sweet Potato Pasta

Prep time: 10 minutes │ Cook time: 20 minutes │ Serves 4

Ingredients:
- 2 large sweet potatoes, peeled
- 1 cup dried figs (about 15 figs), roughly diced
- 1 (8 large slices) package prosciutto, cut into squares
- 1 cup slivered almonds
- 1 cup (4 ounce) container goat cheese, crumbled
- ½ tsp. sea salt
- ½ tbsp. olive oil
- 2 tbsp. water

Directions:
1. Cut the ends off the sweet potatoes and run through a vegetable spiralizer or julienne peeler.
2. Slice the prosciutto into small squares. Then thinly slice the dried figs.
3. Add the olive oil to a large griddle and set over medium heat.
4. Season the potato noodles with sea salt and place in the griddle.
5. Fry for 5-6 minutes, until they become lightly golden and tender, stirring frequently.
6. Transfer to a plate and in the same pan, sauté the sliced prosciutto for 2-3 minutes, stirring frequently.
7. Stir in the slivered almonds and sliced figs and

cook for another 2 minutes until figs are lightly golden and tender.

8. In a small bowl, mix together the goat cheese and water until creamy and add to the potato noodles. Give a stir and remove from the heat.

9. Garnish the dish with the remaining goat cheese and serve hot.

Zucchini Pasta with Pistachio Pesto and Pork

Prep time: 15 minutes | *Total time: 15 minutes* | *Serves 4*

Ingredients:
Pistachio Pesto:
- 2-3 tbsp. olive oil
- 1 ½ cups packed fresh basil
- 1/3 cup pistachios, shelled
- ½ cup packed cilantro
- Zest of ½ a lemon
- ¼ cup Parmesan cheese, freshly grated
- 1 tbsp. water
- Pinch of salt and pepper

For the zoodles:
- 1 ½ tbsp. olive oil, divided
- 4 medium zucchinis
- Salt, to taste

For the pork:
- ½ lb. pork tenderloin
- Salt and pepper, to taste

Directions:
1. Use a vegetable spiralizer to make zucchini noodles. Place the noodles in a colander, season with salt, and let stand for 25-30 minutes.
2. Preheat oven to 450° F.

3. Drizzle the pork with 1-2 tablespoons of olive oil and sprinkle with salt and pepper. Rub with hands until coated.

4. Add the remaining 1 tablespoon olive oil in an oven proof skillet and set over medium/high heat.

5. Place the pork in the skillet and sear for 3 minutes per side, until golden brown.

6. Transfer the skillet to the oven and let roast for 12-15 minutes.

7. Remove from the oven, and let stand for 10 minutes.

8. Add the pistachios to a blender and pulse for a few seconds until roughly chopped.

9. Add the cilantro, basil, parmesan cheese, and lemon zest and pulse until finely chopped.

10. Add water and 2 tablespoons of olive oil and blend for another 15 seconds.

11. Now squeeze the zoodles with hands to remove any extra moisture from them.

12. Place in a large bowl. Pour the pesto sauce over the noodles and stir to combine.

13. Place the pasta into serving plates, top with pork slices, garnish with cheese, and enjoy.

Spiralized Mediterranean Beet and Feta Skillet Bake

Prep time: 5 minutes | Cook time: 5 minutes | Serves 4

Ingredients:

- ½ cup halved yellow cherry tomatoes
- ½ cup halved red cherry tomatoes
- 2 medium garlic cloves, minced
- 2 tbsp. minced fresh parsley, plus 1 teaspoon for garnish
- 1 tbsp. dried oregano
- 1 tbsp. red wine vinegar
- 10 pitted Kalamata olives
- 1 tbsp. extra virgin olive oil
- 2 small beets, peeled and spiralized
- ½ small onion, peeled and spiralized
- Kosher salt and black pepper, to taste
- 4 oz. feta or halloumi cheese, half block cut horizontally

Directions:

1. Preheat the oven to 400° F.
2. Combine all the ingredients in a large bowl except for the cheese and parsley for garnish.
3. Place the cheese in the center of a large oven-safe skillet or casserole dish. Top and surround it with beet noodle mixture.
4. Cover with foil and bake 20 minutes, until the beet noodles wilt.
5. Serve hot garnished with remaining parsley.

Vitamin Bowl

Prep time: 15 minutes │ Total time: 20 minutes │ Serves 3

Ingredients:
- 1 red bell pepper, sliced into thin strips
- ¼ cup green onions, chopped
- 2 carrots, spiralized or julienned
- 1 cup green cabbage, thinly sliced
- 2 medium zucchinis, spiralized or julienned
- ¼ cup cilantro, chopped
- 1 can chickpeas, drained and rinsed
- Salt and pepper, to taste
- Red chili flakes (optional)

For the dressing:
- 1/3 cup tahini
- 3 tbsp. maple syrup
- 1 tbsp. curry powder
- 1 tbsp. fresh grated ginger or 1 tsp dried ginger
- 2 tbsp. lime juice
- 2-3 tbsp.water (as needed)

Directions:

1. In a large salad bowl, combine the red pepper, carrot and zucchini noodles, chickpeas, cabbage, green onions, and cilantro. Season with salt and pepper and red chili flakes, if desire.

2. To make the dressing, in a small bowl, mix the curry powder, maple syrup, ginger, lime juice, and tahini. Add enough water so the mixture gets a thick dressing consistency.

3. Pour the mixture over the vegetables and toss well to coat.

Greek Cucumber Salad

Prep time: 10 minutes | *Serves 1*

Ingredients:

- ½ seedless English cucumber
- ¼ of a green bell pepper, chopped
- 1/3 cup grape tomatoes, halved
- 5 pitted Kalamata olives
- 1 tbsp. red onion, sliced
- Juice of ½ lemon
- 1 oz. fresh feta, sliced
- ½ tbsp. extra virgin olive oil
- Kosher salt and freshly ground black pepper
- ½ tsp. fresh oregano leaves, minced

Directions:

1. Run the cucumber through a vegetable spiral slicer and place on a cutting board. Then chop the noodles into 5 inches long strips, to make them easier to eat.
2. Place the cucumber strands in a large salad work bowl.
3. Add the tomatoes, red onion, bell pepper, and olives.
4. Sprinkle with juice of freshly squeezed lemon.
5. Season with fresh oregano, salt, and pepper and drizzle with ½ of the olive oil. Toss to coat.
6. Place the fresh salad on a serving plate, place a slice of the feta on top, and drizzle with the remaining olive oil. Enjoy.

Cucumber Noodle Salad

Prep time: 10 minutes | *Cook time: 5 minutes* | *Serves 2-3*

Ingredients:

- 3 medium or 2 large cucumbers, spiralized (2 ½ cups noodles)
- 1-1 ½ cups halved cherry or grape tomatoes (about 1 pint)
- 4-6 slices bacon (sugar free), cooked and crumbled
- 1 cup baby spinach, chopped
- 1 tbsp. extra virgin olive oil
- 1 tbsp. fresh lemon juice
- 1/8 tsp. granulated garlic
- ¼ tsp. salt
- Pepper, to taste
- Feta cheese

Directions:

1. Chop the bacon into small cubes and place in a skillet.
2. Let cook for 3-4 minutes, until browned and crispy. Remove from the skillet and set aside.
3. To spiralize the cucumbers, peel them and run through a vegetable spiralizer or julienne peeler.
4. Place the cucumber noodles on the paper towels, cover with another layer of paper towels, and gently press to drain. Transfer to a medium bowl.

5. Add the lemon juice, garlic powder, and pepper, and drizzle with olive oil. Toss to combine.
6. Halve the tomatoes and add to the noodles. Add the chopped spinach and cooked bacon and mix to combine.
7. Sprinkle the dish with crumbled cheese and serve immediately.

Zucchini Mint Pineapple Salad

Prep time: 15 minutes | *Serves 2*

Ingredients:
- 4 cups spiralized zucchini
- 2 cups pineapple, diced into ¼" chunks
- ½ cup sliced mint leaves
- 1 ½ tbsp. high quality olive oil
- Juice of 1 lime (optional)
- ½ tsp. sea salt (optional)

Directions:
1. The spiralized zucchini, pineapple, and mint are prepared.
2. Mix pineapple, zucchini, sliced mint leaves, and olive oil in a large bowl with tongs.
3. Serve immediately and sprinkle on lime juice and sea salt (optional). Enjoy.

Honey Apple Salad with Pecans and Cranberries

Prep time: 15 minutes │ Serves 3

Ingredients:
- 5 cups of baby spinach
- 3 apples, julienned or spiraled
- 1/3 cup dried cranberries
- ½ cup pecans

For the dressing:
- 2 tbsp. extra virgin olive oil
- 1 tbsp. honey
- 1 tbsp. ground Dijon mustard
- Salt and pepper, to taste
- 2 tbsp. balsamic vinegar

Directions:
1. First, start making the dressing. In a small bowl, mix together the olive oil, Dijon mustard, honey, and balsamic vinegar.
2. Season with salt and pepper.
3. Next, in a large salad bowl, combine the julienned apples, baby spinach, pecans, and cranberries.
4. Spoon the dressing over and toss well to coat. Enjoy.

Sweet Potato Noodles with Spinach

Prep time: 10 minutes | *Cook time: 20 minutes* | *Serves 4*

Ingredients:
- 2-pounds sweet potatoes (about 3 potatoes), spiralized
- 1 tbsp. butter
- 2 tbsp. olive oil
- 1 large yellow onion, thinly sliced
- 2-3 garlic cloves, minced
- Pinch of salt
- ¼ cup water
- 1 bag (10-ounces) fresh baby spinach
- Salt and fresh ground pepper, to taste
- ¼ cup chopped fresh parsley
- Grated parmesan cheese

Directions:
1. Peel the potatoes and run through a spiralizer. Place in a large bowl and set aside.
2. Add the olive oil and butter to a large pan and set over medium-high heat.
3. Once the butter is melted and the [pan is very hot, throw in the onions, garlic, season with a pinch of salt and cook for 2-3 minutes, until the onions are just tender.
4. Add the potato spirals and cook for about 7-9 minutes, stirring frequently, until the noodles soften.

5. Pour about ¼ cup of water into the pan and continue cooking for another 2-4 minutes, until the potatoes are cooked through and light golden.

6. Add the spinach, season with salt and pepper and toss to combine. When the spinach wilts, remove the pan from the heat.

7. Sprinkle with chopped parsley and cheese and serve immediately.

Zucchini Noodles With Bacon, Ricotta and Peas

Prep time: 10 minutes | Cook time: 5 minutes | Serves 4

Ingredients:

- 2 large zucchini, spiralized
- 3 slices of bacon
- ½ cup part skim ricotta cheese
- ½ cup frozen peas, thawed
- 1 tbsp. fresh basil, chopped
- 2 tsp. extra virgin olive oil
- 1/8 tsp. garlic powder
- Salt and pepper, to taste

Directions:

1. Add the bacon slices to a skillet and fry until golden brown on both sides. Remove from the skillet and let them cool.
2. Add the olive oil to a large pan and set over medium high heat.
3. Add the zucchini noodles, season with garlic powder, salt and pepper and cook for 1-2 minutes until heated through. Remove the pan from the heat.
4. Break the fried bacon into pieces and add to the zucchini noodles along with peas, ricotta and chopped basil. Adjust seasonings as needed. Enjoy.

Easy Roasted Garlic-Parmesan Potato Noodles

Prep time: 10 minutes | Cook time: 15 minutes | Serves 6

Ingredients:
- 2 lbs. red potatoes, spiralized
- 1 tbsp. extra virgin olive oil
- Salt and pepper, to taste
- ½ tsp. garlic powder
- ½ tbsp. parmesan cheese, grated
- 2 tbsp. parsley, chopped (for garnish)

Directions:
1. Preheat the oven to 425 F.
2. Peel your potatoes and pass through a spiralizer. Place in a large bowl.
3. Drizzle with olive oil and season with salt, pepper and garlic powder. Toss well with your hands and transfer to a large baking dish lined with parchment.
4. Bake in the oven for about 15 minutes or until they are about to brown.
5. Turn on the broiler. Remove the noodles from the oven and sprinkle with grated Parmezan.
6. Place the roasted noodles in a serving bowl, garnish with freshly chopped parsley and serve.

Vegetable Noodles with Cabbage

Prep time: 15 minutes | *Cook time: 6 minutes* | *Serves 2-3*

Ingredients:

- 2-3 zucchini and/or yellow squash, spiralized
- 2 handfuls of chopped napa cabbage
- 1 shallot or 2-3 tbsp. chopped red onion
- 1 tbsp. sesame oil
- 2-3 tbsp. creamy cashew butter
- ½ to 1 tsp. red chili flakes
- 2 tbsp. tamari or gluten free soy sauce
- 1 tsp. honey
- 1 tsp. garlic (minced)
- ¼ tsp. five spices Asian seasoning
- Dash of sea salt
- Black pepper, to taste

Directions:

1. Peel the zucchini and squash and run through a spiralizer. Then chop the onion and cabbage.
2. Add the sesame oil, cashew butter, tamari, chili flakes, and garlic to large frying pan and set over medium-high heat.
3. Add the zucchini and squash noodles, followed by honey, five spices, sea salt and pepper.
4. Toss well to combine and cook for 3-4 minutes, stirring occasionally, until veggies become tender.

5. Remove from the heat and sprinkle with red chili flakes.
6. Serve hot or at room temperature.
7. Great to be served with chicken or beef.

Spicy Butternut Squash Noodles with Apples, Lentils and Nuts

Prep time: 15 minutes | *Cook time: 6 minutes* | *Serves 4*

Ingredients:
- 4 tsp. maple syrup
- 1 tbsp. lemon juice
- 2 tsp. balsamic vinegar
- 7 oz. butternut squash, peeled, spiralized
- 1 big Golden Delicious apple
- 2 tsp. vegetable oil
- 1 garlic clove, minced (1 tsp.)
- 1 ½ cups cooked French green lentils
- 2 tbsp. fresh parsley, chopped
- ¼ cup chopped dried cranberries, optional
- ¼ cup chopped toasted walnuts, pecans, or hazelnuts

Directions:
1. To make the dressing, in a small cup combine the lemon juice, maple syrup, and balsamic vinegar. Set aside.
2. Then, peel and spiralize the butternut squash and apple into thin noodles.
3. Add the vegetable oil to a large pan and set over medium-high heat.
4. Throw in the squash noodles, season with salt, and let them cook for 2 minutes.

5. Next, add the apple noodles and give a stir. After a minute, add the garlic and cook about 25-30 seconds, until the noodles are tender.

6. Stir in the cooked lentils and season with salt. Pour the prepared maple mixture over and toss well to coat.

7. Remove the pan from the heat. Place the noodles in a large serving bowl, sprinkle with chopped parsley, cranberries and nuts and serve.

Mexican Sweet Potato Rice

Prep time: 10 minutes | Cook time: 10 minutes | Serves 6

Ingredients:

- 2 large sweet potatoes, peeled, spiralized
- 1 tsp. canola oil
- 1 cup black beans, drained and rinsed
- 1 cup canned corn, drained
- ½ cup vegetable broth
- ¼ cup chopped fresh cilantro
- 1 lime, juiced
- ¼ tsp. salt
- 1 plum tomato, seeded, chopped

Directions:

1. Using a vegetable spiralizer, slice the sweet potatoes into noodles and place on a cutting board. Using a chef's knife, thinly chop them into rice size pieces.
2. Add the canola oil to a non-stick skillet and set over medium heat. When it begins to sizzle, throw in the beans, potatoes, corn, and chopped cilantro.
3. Let them cook for a minute, and then add the vegetable broth and lime juice. Season with salt, stir well and cook for another 3-5 minutes, stirring occasionally, until all liquid is absorbed and the potatoes have softened.
4. Garnish the dish with thinly sliced tomatoes and serve.

Mouthwatering Salad with Roasted Corn and Zucchini Noodles

Prep time: 10 minutes | Cook time: 10 minutes | Serves 6

Ingredients:
- ½ large red onion, diced
- 2 ears of corn
- 2 large zucchini, spiralized
- Salt and pepper to season corn

Dressing:
- ½ tsp. pepper
- 1 tbsp. olive oil
- Juice and zest of 1 lime
- ½ tbsp. apple cider vinegar
- 1 tsp. honey
- ½ tsp. chili powder
- ¾ tsp. salt
- 1 tsp. garlic powder

Directions:
1. Prepare the outdoor grill.
2. Shuck the corn, coat with cooking spray and sprinkle with salt and pepper.
3. Grill for a couple of minutes, until charred, turning halfway through grilling. Once the corn is done, remove from the grill and let it cool.
4. In the meantime start making the dressing by

combining olive oil, lime juice and zest, honey, vinegar, chili powder, garlic powder, salt and pepper in a small bowl.

5. Slice the zucchini into thin noodles and place in a large bowl. Add the red onion and cheese, pour the dressing over and toss to combine.

6. Cut the kernels from the cob and add to the top of the salad. Enjoy.

Pear, Pomegranate and Roasted Butternut Squash Salad with Maple Sesame Vinaigrette

Prep time: 25 minutes | Cook time: 10 minutes | Serves 3

Ingredients:
- 1 medium butternut squash, spiralized
- ¾ cup walnuts, roughly chopped
- Salt and pepper, to taste
- 1 large pear
- 5 oz. container of arugula
- ¾ cup pomegranate seeds

Dressing:
- 1 tbsp. real maple syrup
- 2 tbsp. apple cider vinegar
- 1 tbsp. extra virgin olive oil
- 1 tbsp. sesame oil
- 1 garlic clove, minced
- 1 tsp. white sesame seeds
- 1 tbsp. soy sauce
- Pepper, to taste

Directions:

1. Preheat oven to 400 F. Peel the butternut squash, and using a spiralizer, slice it into noodles and spread out in a baking sheet, lined with parchment paper.
2. Season with salt and pepper, drizzle with cooking oil and bake in the oven for about 10 minutes, until just tender.
3. Meanwhile, in a small bowl, mix the maple syrup, olive oil, sesame oil, vinegar, sesame seeds, soy sauce, garlic, and pepper and set aside.
4. Run the pear through a spiralizer and place in a large salad bowl, with chopped walnuts and arugula.
5. Remove the done noodles from the oven, let them cool slightly, and add to the salad bowl.
6. Pour the prepared dressing over and toss well to coat.
7. Serve and enjoy.

Potato and Zucchini Noodles with Chickpeas

Prep time: 5 minutes | Cook time: 25 minutes | Serves 3

Ingredients:

For roasted chickpeas:
- 1 can chickpeas, drained
- ½ tsp. garlic powder
- 1 tbsp. extra virgin olive oil
- Salt and pepper, to taste

For veggie noodles:
- 1 medium sweet potato
- 2 zucchini
- 1 tbsp. olive oil
- 1 tbsp. water
- 2 tbsp. of your favorite pesto
- 1 tsp. minced garlic

Directions:
1. Preheat oven to 425 F.
2. Drain the chickpeas in a colander and place in a baking dish, spreading them in an even layer.
3. Drizzle with olive oil, season with salt, pepper and garlic powder and bake them in the oven for about half an hour. During the roasting, flip them 2-3 times to roast evenly.

4. Meanwhile, run the zucchini and sweet potato through spiralizer.
5. Add 1 tablespoon of olive oil to a skillet and set over medium heat. Add the garlic and cook for 15 seconds. Then add the sweet potatoes, followed by 1 tablespoon of water and cook for 5-6 minutes, covered.
6. Throw in the zucchini spirals and allow to cook for another 2-3 minutes. Finally stir in the pesto and remove the skillet from the heat.
7. Divide the noodles among serving plates, top with chickpeas and serve.

Prosciutto Wrapped Tasty Rolls

Prep time: 15 minutes | Cook time: 5 minutes | Serves 6

Ingredients:
- 1 large sweet potato, peeled, spiralized
- 12 slices of prosciutto, sliced in half
- 3 tbsp. goat cheese
- 6 dates, pitted, sliced thinly
- ½ cup chopped pecans
- Olive oil

For the maple-balsamic:
- ¼ cup maple syrup
- 3 tbsp. balsamic vinegar
- 2 tsp. Dijon mustard

Directions:
1. Add the olive oil to a large frying pan and set over medium heat. Once the pan is very hot, add the potato spirals and season with salt and pepper.
2. Put the lid on the pan and let the noodles cook for 5-6 minutes, until they are cooked through. Using a apatula, gently toss occasionally to prevent sticking to the bottom.
3. Meanwhile, combine the maple syrup and vinegar in a small saucepan and bring to a boil over medium high heat. Then reduce the heat to low and let it simmer, stirring occasionally until

the mixture has reduced to 1/3 cup. Set aside.

4. Place two pieces of prosciutto and sprinkle with ½ tablespoon of goat cheese, followed by 1sliced date and 1 tablespoons of pecans. Then top with a thin layer of sweet potato noodles. Gently roll the prosciutto to make a parcel.

5. Using a sharp knife, cut in halve and secure each part with a toothpick.

6. In this way, roll the remaining prosciutto so you get 6 rolls. Place them in a serving plate, drizzle with the prepared maple-balsamic sauce and serve.

Creamy Chicken Zucchini Fettuccine

Prep time: 10 minutes | Cook time: 15 minutes | Serves 2-3

Ingredients:

- 1 small onion, chopped
- 2-3 large zucchinis, peeled, spiralized
- 1 lb. (450 g) leftover cooked chicken, chopped
- ½ tsp. fine sea salt
- ½ tsp. freshly cracked black pepper
- 1 large head (21 oz.) cauliflower, roughly chopped
- 2 cups chicken broth
- 2 garlic cloves, minced
- 2 tbsp. nutritional yeast
- 1 tbsp. Dijon mustard
- 2 tbsp. white balsamic vinegar
- ½ lime juice
- 1 tsp. capers
- 8 oz. mushrooms, sliced

Directions:

1. To make zucchini fettuccine, run the peeled zucchini through a vegetable spiralizer or mandolin, slicing them into fettuccine like ribbons.
2. Coat a skillet with cooking spray and place over medium heat. Add the garlic, onion, salt and pepper to the pan and sauté for 1-2 minutes, until the onions become tender.
3. Add the cauliflower and continue cooking for

another 1-2 minutes.

4. Pour in the chicken broth and continue cooking, covered.

5. Once it begins to boil, turn down the heat and let it simmer, until the cauliflower has softened, about 7 minutes.

6. Meanwhile, place the mushrooms in a large frying pan and cook until golden brown.

7. Finally, add the chicken and cook over medium-low heat until heated through. Set aside.

8. Combine the Dijon mustard, lime juice, balsamic vinegar, and nutritional yeast in a blender; add the cauliflower mixture and pulse, until smooth and creamy.

9. Add the capers and pulse 3-4 times, until just blended.

10. Add the cauliflower mixture to the pan with mushrooms and reserved chicken and let simmer over low-medium heat.

11. Place the zucchini noodles into serving plates and top with the chicken sauce.

12. This prepared hot chicken sauce will soften the zucchini noodles, but to have even softer paste, you can cook it in the chicken sauce for 2-3 minutes.

13. Sprinkle the dish with chopped cilantro and serve.

Healthy Veggie Noodle and Chickpea Salad

Prep time: 15 minutes | Cook time: 20 minutes | Serves 3

Ingredients:
- ¼ cup green onions, chopped
- 1 red bell pepper, cut into thin strips
- 2 carrots, spiralized or julienned
- 1 cup green cabbage, thinly sliced
- 2 medium zucchinis, spiralized or julienned
- ¼ cup cilantro, chopped
- 2 tbsp. lime juice
- 1 can chickpeas, drained
- 1 tbsp. curry powder
- Salt and pepper, to taste
- Red chili flakes (optional)

Dressing:
- 1/3 cup tahini
- 3 tbsp. maple syrup
- 1 tbsp. fresh grated ginger or 1 tsp. dried ginger
- 2-3 tbsp. water (as needed)

Directions:

1. In a large salad bowl, combine the red pepper, spiralized carrots and zucchinis, chickpeas, cabbage, green onions, cilantro; season with salt and pepper and red chilli flakes, if desired.

2. To make the dressing, in a small bowl, mix the curry powder, maple syrup, ginger, lime juice and tahini. Add enough water so the mixture gets a thick dressing consistency.

3. Pour the mixture over the vegetables and toss well to coat.

Spicy Sweet Potato Noodle Pancakes

Prep time: 5 minutes | Cook time: 15 minutes | Serves 4

Ingredients:

- 2 medium (375 g) sweet potatoes, spiralized
- 2 eggs
- ¼ cup pecans
- ½ tsp. nutmeg
- 1 tsp. cinnamon
- ½ tsp. olive oil
- Salt and pepper, to taste
- 1 cup non-fat Greek yogurt
- 2 baby nectarines, diced
- 4 tbsp. maple syrup
- Olive oil cooking spray

Directions:

1. Add the olive oil to a large frying pan and set over medium-low heat.
2. Add the sweet potato noodles, salt, and pepper and let cook, until potato spirals are tender, about 7-8 minutes, stirring frequently.
3. Sprinkle with nutmeg and cinnamon, stir, and remove the pan from the heat.
4. Transfer the noodles into a large mixing bowl. Crack in the eggs and mix well to coat.
5. Coat a large pan with cooking spray and set over medium-low heat.

6. Add a handful of the potato noodles to the pan and let cook 3-4 minutes. Then flip over to fry the other side, about 2 minutes. Repeat with the remaining noodles.

7. Place the done pancakes into serving plates. Add ¼ cup yogurt on top of each, then garnish with nectarine slices and pecans and drizzle with maple syrup. Enjoy.

Spiralizer Sweet Potato with Caramelized Onion, Goat Cheese and Pine Nuts

Prep time: 15 minutes | Cook time: 20 minutes | Serves 4

Ingredients:

- 1 large yellow onion, sliced
- 12 oz. (350 g) raw sweet potatoes, spiralized
- ½ tbsp. butter
- Pinch of sugar
- 2 tbsp. pine nuts
- Salt and pepper, to taste
- 2 oz. (60 g) goat cheese, crumbled
- 1 tbsp. fresh thyme leaves (for garnish)
- 1/3 cup vegetable stock (optional)

Directions:

1. Preheat the oven to 400 °F.
2. Add ½ tablespoon of butter and ½ tablespoon of olive oil to a frying pan and set over medium heat.
3. Once hot, add the onions to the pan, sprinkle with salt, pepper, and a pinch of sugar and stir to combine.
4. Then turn down the heat to low and let the onions cook over low heat, stirring frequently.
5. Meanwhile, place the spiralized potatoes in a large bowl, drizzle with 1 tablespoon of olive oil, then salt and pepper to taste.

6. Line a baking sheet with parchment and place the noodles onto it.
7. Transfer to the oven and bake for 10 minutes. Then flip over with hands and continue baking for another 5 minutes.
8. And during this time, stir onions to avoid burning. If they look too dry, add 1-2 tablespoons of vegetable broth to deglaze the pan.
9. When the potatoes are tender, place in a serving dish and top with the caramelized onions and goat cheese.
10. Sprinkle with pine nuts and fresh thyme. Enjoy.

Zucchini Noodles with Cilantro Lime Chicken

Prep time: 10 minutes | Cook time: 12 minutes | Serves 12

Ingredients:
- 3 large zucchini
- ½ tsp. cumin
- 1 tsp. salt
- ¼ tsp, ground black pepper
- ½ lbs, boneless, skinless chicken breasts, cut into small pieces
- 2 tsp. any small hot pepper/jalapeño or to taste, seeded and minced
- ½ large lime juice
- ¾ cup cilantro, chopped
- Cooking spray

Directions:
1. To make zucchini noodles, run your zucchinis through a vegetable spiral slicer or use a julienne peeler or mandolin. Place in a bowl and set aside.
2. Coat a large frying pan with cooking spray and set over medium-high heat.
3. Add the chicken and cook, stirring occasionally, until golden brown.
4. Season with ½ tsp salt, ground black pepper, and cumin, stir, and remove the chicken from the pan.

5. Rinse the pan and place back over the heat. Gently coat with cooking spray and add the zucchini noodles to the pan. Let cook for 2-3 minutes until the noodles become tender.

6. Remove the pan from the heat. Toss in the browned chicken, jalapenos, drizzle with lemon juice, sprinkle with the remaining ½ teaspoon of salt and cilantro, and stir well to combine.

7. Serve immediately.

Chicken Cucumber Noodles

Prep time: 15 minutes Cook time: 15 to 20 minutes │Serves 4

Ingredients:
- 2 cucumbers, spiralized
- 2 tsp. olive oil
- 4 (6 ounces) boneless, skinless chicken breast, cut into 1-inch pieces
- ½ tsp. Himalayan pink salt
- 2 cups tomato-basil pasta sauce
- ¼ cup Kalamata olives, pitted and coarsely chopped
- 1 tbsp. capers
- ¼ tsp. red pepper, crushed
- ¼ cup (1 ounces) Parmesan cheese, shredded
- Chopped fresh basil (for garnish)

Directions:
1. Run the cucumbers through a spiralizer and place into a medium bowl.
2. Add the oil to a skillet and set over medium-high heat. Season the chicken with salt and add to the pan. Let it cook until golden brown, 5-7 minutes.
3. Stir in the pasta sauce, olives, capers, and crushed red pepper and bring the mixture to a simmer, about 5 minutes, or until the chicken is cooked through.

4. Divide the cucumber noodles between 4 serving plates and place about 1 ½ cup fried chicken mixture on top.

5. Sprinkle the dish with 1 tablespoon of Parmesan cheese and chopped fresh basil leaves. Enjoy.

Spicy Chicken Soup with Zucchini Noodles

Prep time: 15 minutes | *Cook time: 30 minutes* | *Serves 6*

Ingredients:
- 2 zucchini, spiralized
- 12 ounces (360 g) of chicken breast, cut into bite-sized pieces
- 5 cups vegetable broth
- ¼ cup bamboo shoots
- 1 small organic lemon, juiced and zested
- 1 red chili, finely chopped
- 1 cup white button mushrooms, cut into halves
- 2 purple onions, sliced
- 2 tbsp. ginger, grated
- 2 tbsp. soy sauce
- 2 tbsp. sake or white wine
- 1 tbsp. white wine vinegar
- 1 tsp. curry powder
- 1 tsp. turmeric powder or freshly grated turmeric
- 2 tbsp. cooking oil
- Salt and pepper, to taste

Directions:

1. Pass the zucchini through a spiralizer to make noodles.
2. Add the cooking oil to a large skillet and set over medium heat.
3. Add the turmeric, chilli, ginger, curry powder, salt and pepper and stir-fry for about 1 minute.
4. Then, place the chicken pieces in the pan and cook for 4-5 minutes per side, until they acquire a golden crust.
5. Next, stir in the onions, mushrooms, zucchini noodles, and bamboo shoots. Sauté for 5 minutes.
6. Finally, add the soy sauce, lemon, sake, and vegetable broth and cook for about 25 minutes, covered, until the vegetables are soft.

Summer Tuna Salad with Cucumber Sesame Noodles

Prep time: 15 minutes | *Cook time: 10 minutes* | *Serves 6*

Ingredients:

- 4 cucumbers, spiralized (or peeled)
- 10 ounces (300 g) canned tuna, drained
- 2 small purple onions, chopped
- 3 tbsp. sesame seeds
- 1 inch fresh root ginger, minced or grated
- 2 celery stalks, chopped
- ¼ cup (5 g) chopped parsley
- 1 tbsp. dried thyme
- 4 tbsp. red wine vinegar
- 2 tbsp. soy sauce
- 2 tbsp. olive oil
- 1 tsp. chilli powder or hot pepper sauce
- Salt and black pepper, to taste

Directions:

1. Make cucumber noodles using a spiralizer or a julienne peeler. Set aside.
2. To make the dressing, combine the soy sauce, dried thyme, red wine vinegar, and chilli powder in a mixing bowl. Then mix in the olive oil, a little at a time, until a thick and smooth consistency is achieved. Set aside.
3. In a large serving bowl, combine the cucumber noodles, tuna, onions, ginger, chopped celery, and parsley. Pour the dressing over and toss to combine.
4. Sprinkle the salad with sesame seeds and serve.

Zucchini Noodles with Bacon and Gouda Cheese

Prep time: 10 minutes | *Cook time: 10 minutes* | *Serves 4*

Ingredients:
- 4 large zucchini, spiralized
- 12 oz. cooked ham, diced
- 8 oz. of Gouda cheese, grated
- 1 garlic clove, finely chopped
- 1 cup soft cheese
- 2 tbsp. oregano or mixed Italian herbs
- 1 tbsp. olive oil
- Salt and pepper, to taste

Directions:
1. Using a spiralizer, spiralize the zucchini and place in a medium bowl and set aside.
2. Add the olive oil to a large skillet and set over medium heat.
3. Once the oil is hot, add the garlic and ham and cook for 2-3 minutes, until the ham is lightly browned.
4. Add the zucchini spirals and sauté for 2 minutes.
5. Stir in soft cheese and Italian herbs and cook for another 5 minutes, stirring occasionally.
6. Place the zucchini mixture into a serving dish, sprinkle with grated cheese, and serve.

Beef Ragu Zoodles

Prep time: 5 minutes | *Cook time: 25 minutes* | *Serves 4*

Ingredients:
- 1 ½ lbs. (680 g) grass fed ground beef
- ½ cup (125 g) red pesto
- 2 tbsp. butter, divided
- Bunch of fresh parsley
- ½ tsp. Himalayan pink salt
- 4 medium fresh zucchini, spiralized

Directions:
1. Melt 1 tablespoon butter in a saucepan over medium high heat.
2. Add ground beef and cook about 5 to 8 minutes until brown, stirring frequently.
3. Stir in the red pesto and fresh chopped parsley. Turn down the heat to low and cook for at least 2 minutes. Turn off the heat and transfer the ground beef mixture to a bowl.
4. To make zucchini noodles pass the zucchini through a spiralizer or use a julienne peeler.
5. Heat the remaining 1 tablespoon butter in a saucepan over medium-high heat. Add the zoodles and stir-fry for 2-3 minutes or until al dente.
6. Transfer to the ground beef mixture and mix well to combine.
7. Serve and enjoy!

Spiralized Cucumber Sesame Salad

Prep time: 10 minutes | Serves 2-4

Ingredients:
- 2 cucumbers, spiralized
- 2 tbsp. rice vinegar
- 2 tbsp. sesame oil, toasted
- 1 tbsp. honey
- ¼ tsp. red chili flakes
- 1 tsp. salt
- Sesame seeds, toasted
- Green onions, sliced (for garnish)

Directions:
1. Mix sesame oil, rice vinegar, honey, salt, and red chili flakes in a medium bowl.
2. Add spiralized cucumbers.
3. Top with sesame seeds and green onions.
4. Enjoy!

Super Healthy Green Ribbon Salad

Prep time: 15 minutes │ Cook time: 20 minutes │ Serves 6

Ingredients:
- 4 cup kale, torn
- 2 medium zucchini
- 4 cup spinach leaves
- 1 green apple
- ½ tsp. sea salt
- 1 tbsp. white balsamic vinegar
- 1 tbsp. olive oil
- 1 tbsp. grade B maple syrup

Directions:
1. Thoroughly wash the kale and spinach and wrap in a clean kitchen towel to dry.
2. Then roll the leaves together, burrito style, and cut into ribbons, using a sharp knife. Transfer to a large salad bowl.
3. Next, core the apple, thinly slice it, and add to the salad bowl. Using a vegetable spiralizer, slice the zucchini into ribbons and add to the bowl.
4. In a small bowl, combine the olive oil, white balsamic vinegar, maple syrup. Season with sea salt.
5. Pour the dressing over the salad and toss well to combine.

Tuna and Zucchini Noodles

Prep time: 15 minutes | *Cook time: 10 minutes* | *Serves 6*

Ingredients:

- 1 tbsp. olive oil
- 4 large zucchini, spiralized
- 2 sage leaves, chopped
- 1 carrot, spiralized
- 1 tbsp. cooking oil
- 7 oz. (210 g) canned tuna, preferably without oil
- 3 tbsp. canned capers, drained, halved
- 1 organic lemon, juiced
- 2 tbsp. Dijon mustard
- 1 tbsp. rosemary, chopped
- Black pepper, to taste
- 4 egg yolks
- Pinch of chilli flakes

Directions:

1. Run the zucchini and carrot through a spiralizer and place in a bowl. Set aside.
2. Add the cooking oil to a large saucepan and set over medium heat.
3. Once the oil is heated, add the vegetable spirals and sauté for a few minutes. Transfer noodles to serving plates.
4. Add sage, rosemary, and chilli flakes to the same pan and sauté for a minute.
5. Stir in the capers, tuna, and lemon juice and cook for another 5 minutes.
6. Remove from the heat.
7. In a small bowl, mix mustard and yolks together. Gradually add the olive oil, a little at a time, and mix to achieve a smooth, creamy texture. Mix in the fried sage and rosemary and whisk.
8. Place the vegetable pasta into individual plates. Top with sauce, cooked tuna, and capers. Enjoy.

Butternut Squash "Fettucine"

Prep time: 15 minutes | Cook time: 5 minutes | Serves 2

Ingredients:

- 1 small butternut squash, peeled, spiraled
- ½ tbsp. extra virgin olive oil
- Black pepper, to taste
- 3 slices thick-cut bacon, cubed
- 2 cups curly kale, finely chopped
- ¼ cup goat cheese, crumbled
- Salt, to taste
- 1 large garlic clove, sliced thinly

Directions:

1. Preheat the oven to 400°F.
2. Run the butternut squash through a vegetable spiralizer and place on a baking dish lined with parchment.
3. Sprinkle with black pepper and olive oil and roast in the oven for about 10 minutes or until al dente.
4. Add the diced bacon to a frying pan and set over medium heat. Cook for about 5 minutes per side, until golden brown and crispy.
5. Using a slotted spoon, transfer the bacon to a plate. Remove about half of the bacon fat from the pan.

6. Add the garlic and kale to the pan, season with salt and pepper, and sauté for 4-5 minutes until the greens wilt.

7. Place the squash noodles in 2 serving bowls, top with cooked kale and bacon, sprinkle with goat cheese. Enjoy.

Spinach Garlic Frittata

Prep time: 10 minutes | *Cook time: 20 minutes* | *Serves 4*

Ingredients:
- 1 zucchini, thinly sliced into noodles
- 3 eggs, beaten
- 9 egg whites + (or 12 egg whites)
- 2 oz. (60 g) goat cheese, crumbled
- 3 cups spinach
- Pinch of garlic powder
- Salt and pepper, to taste

Directions:
1. Preheat the oven to 375 °F.
2. Coat a frying pan with cooking spray and set on the stove.
3. Add the spinach to the pan, season with a pinch of garlic, and let it cook, covered, until wilted.
4. Place a thin layer of spinach on the bottom of the pan, add zucchini noodles on top, then finish with the remaining spinach. Season the greens with salt and pepper.
5. Pour the beaten eggs over.
6. After 2-3 minutes, add the crumbled goat cheese and using a wooden spatula, spread and push cheese pieces into the cooking eggs.
7. Once the edges are set and golden, transfer the pan to the oven and bake for approximately 15 minutes.
8. When the eggs are set and the bottom becomes light golden, remove the frittata from the oven.

Parsnip Noodles with Ginger Garlic Dressing

Prep time: 10 minutes | Cook time: 7 minutes | Serves 4

Ingredients:
- 6 medium parsnips, peeled and trimmed
- 3 tbsp. extra virgin olive oil
- 3 tbsp. coconut aminos
- Gluten free fish sauce to taste
- 1 large lime, juiced
- 1 ½ tsp. garlic powder
- 1 tbsp. ground ginger
- 4 green onions, chopped
- ½ tbsp. coconut oil (optional)

Directions:
1. To make noodles, run your parsnips through a spiral slicer with the thinnest blade. Set aside.
2. If you prefer to cook parsnips, heat ½ tablespoon coconut oil in a large frying pan over medium to low heat.
3. Add the parsnip noodles and let cook for 6-7 minutes, covered, until they are crisp tender.
4. To make the dressing, combine the olive oil, fish sauce, garlic, lime juice, coconut aminos, and ginger in a small bowl.
5. Stir well and pour the dressing over the noodles. Toss to coat.
6. Divide the noodles between serving plates, garnish with green onions, and serve.

Carrot Pasta with Mushroom Sauce

Prep time: 10 minutes | Cook time: 15 minutes | Serves 2

Ingredients:
- 3 large carrots, spiraled
- ¾ cup chopped mushrooms, any kind
- 2 tbsp. shallots, chopped
- 3 tsp. olive oil
- ¼ tsp. dried basil
- 2 large garlic clove, minced
- Pinch black pepper
- Pinch of salt

Directions:
1. Using a spiralizer, slice the carrots into noodles and set aside.
2. Add the olive oil to a large saucepan and place over moderate heat.
3. Add the shallots and garlic to the saucepan and cook for 3-4 minutes until tender and golden brown.
4. Next, add the chopped mushrooms and cook for 5-6 minutes, stirring frequently. Season with salt and pepper.
5. Add the carrot noodles, stir, and continue cooking for another 7-10 minutes until the carrots soften.
6. Enjoy.

Conclusion

I hope you enjoyed the many recipes you found! The next step is to pick up a spiralizer today, if you have not already, and begin transforming your vegetables from dull and bland to pasta imitators that are healthy and delicious. You will not regret adding spiralized vegetables to your diet. They are nutritious and your body will thank you for them.

Finally, if you enjoyed the recipes and information you found in this book, then I wouldd like to ask you for a favor. Would you be kind enough to leave a review for this book on Amazon? It would be greatly appreciated!

Thank you for reading!